Name Gemma

Job Senior Research Funding Manager

'When I was young I really enjoyed figuring out why or how things happened, particularly with the human body, and the more I found out, the more interesting it became.'

Fave fact:

'An adult is made up of around 7,000, 000,000,000,000,000,000,000,000 (7 octillion) atoms!'

Name Buddhini

Job Science Communications Manager

'I translate science into English so that people without a science background can understand and get excited about it.'

Fave fact:

'The way DNA is packaged in our cells is a bit like if you had to pack the whole of the London underground into a suitcase.'

Contents

Be safe

You should be able to have a go at everything in your *Brownie Annual*, but sometimes it is a good idea to get some help. When you see this symbol, ask an adult if they can lend a hand.

Web safe

This symbol means you should follow your Brownie Web Safe Code. To remember it, look at page 15 in your *Brownie Adventures* book.

Badges!
Look out for this sign. If you enjoyed the activity on that page, you might like to try the badge too!

WE DISCOVER, WE GROW
Girlguiding

Published by Girlguiding
17–19 Buckingham Palace Road
London SW1W 0PT
info@girlguiding.org.uk
www.girlguiding.org.uk

© Girlguiding 2015
Registered charity number 306016.
Incorporated by Royal Charter.

ISBN 978-0-85260-256-0
Girlguiding order code 6005

Printed and bound in Italy by L.E.G.O. S.p.A.

Editor: Jessica Feehan
Writers: Rosie Fletcher, Alison Griffiths, Francesca Jones, Mariano Kälfors, Daniel McKeown, Bryony Pemberton, Nithya Rae, Ellen Reid, Ruth Stone, Helen Thomas, Emma Ward
Design Manager: David Jones
Cover Designer: Yuan Zhuang
Designers: Angie Daniel, Helen Davis, Andrew Smith, Yuan Zhuang
Production Controller: Wendy Reynolds
Photographers: Gemma Huntingford, Amy Smirk
Brownie Programme Adviser: Katharine Lee

Illustrations courtesy of Shutterstock unless otherwise stated. Photography © Girlguiding unless otherwise stated.

Girlguiding would like to thank the following units for their help with this Annual: 1st Bantaskin Brownies, 4th Belmont Brownies, 1st Forest Hill Brownies, 1st Rawcliffe (St Mark's) Brownies,

3rd Writtle Brownies.
Users are reminded that during the lifespan of this publication there may be changes to:
• Girlguiding's policy
• legal requirements
• practice by governing bodies
• British Standards
which will affect the accuracy of the information contained within these pages.

Although the terms 'parent' and 'daughter' are used in this resource, users should remember that what is said may apply to a carer or other adult with parental responsibility, or their ward.

FSC
MIX
Paper from responsible sources
FSC® C023419
www.fsc.org

You can do anything

Badge-tastic

Last year we asked you to invent a new Brownie badge for something you care about, and you sent us LOADS of fantastic designs.

Photo gallery

We wish we could put all your badges on this page, but sadly there's room for only a few. Here they are!

Welcome to the 2016 _Brownie Annual_! You may not know this, but each year your Annual is inspired by you and your Brownie friends. Here's how this year's came about...

Secret science

Which brings us to this year's Annual. Did you know that all of the things you told us you care about involve science in some way, however small? Animal care? Science! Sporty stuff? Science! Baking delicious food? Science! So in these pages you can find out about all the amazing science stuff that goes on around you every day – and have a whole load of fun in the process. What's not to love?

Winners!

Meet our winners of the *2015 Brownie Annual* badge design competition.

Overall winner: Summer, 1st Brierley Hill Brownies ('I've conquered my fear')

You category: Anna, 2nd Beccles Brownies (Money)

Community category: Emma, 1st Eldwick Brownies (Carer)

World category: Abigail, 4th St Neots Brownies (Fair trade)

Community category

carer

Overall winner

Money

bank of england
Twenty
pound 2015
10p
2p £1

You category

Fair Trade

World category

You can do it!

This badge design summed it all up (bravo, Josephine from 2nd Southfields Brownies!). You can do absolutely anything you put your mind to, and Brownies is all about finding out what that is.

Detective Brownie: An ex-CAT science

Scruff isn't acting like his usual doggy self – what shadow is he casting?

The detective business was quiet. Like a poorly organised airline, I didn't have any cases. I was keeping myself amused on a Brownie Day Out to the local university's Science Department with Scruff, my dog deputy, and Sophie, my human deputy. Something about Scruff was off, like milk left out on the doorstep or a television that's not on.

'Come on DB, we'll get left behind!' Sophie turned back from the group. I was trying to stop Scruff going for the tuna sandwiches in my backpack.

'It's Scruff, kid. He's not looking too hot.' He sat up with his tail wrapped around him, his ears sticking up, licking his paws. Odd for a dog. But not odd for…

Illustrated by Rémy Simard

...a cat!' Sophie was not wrong. Scruff was acting just like a cat.

'You could say he's not "feline" well.' Scruff had crumbs of food around his mouth. This called for further investigation. We were right next to some of the labs and I knew the answer to Scruff's behaviour would be in there.

'You can open the door only with the right fingerprint.' I looked closely. There were smudges on the shiny fingerprint scanner. 'We've just got to pick the right one.'

Can you find the right match for the fingerprint?

A   B   C

The door swung open and we were into the first lab. It was empty. Scruff stretched and yawned. I might have bet my badges he almost meowed.

'Look DB!' Sophie pointed to another door labelled 'TOP SECRET RESEARCH PROJECT'.

'Why has it always got to be Top Secret Research Projects?' I sighed. There was a number pad next to the door. Who was to say what the code was? I looked at Scruff. He coughed up a hairball.

'Might as well start with the obvious,' I muttered, plugging a lollipop into the corner of my mouth.

Turn the word DOGCAT into a number by using the letters and numbers of a phone's keypad

The door slid open. Sophie looked as stunned as I felt.

'What can I say, kid? I'm a very good detective.'

It was pitch-dark inside. I pulled a torch from my backpack and found the box that held the circuit for the lights. Some of the wires needed putting back in place, but I'm a detective, so I'm good at making the right connections.

Detective Brownie and Sophie need to connect the right wire to complete the circuit – which wire should they connect?

I flicked the switch. The lights came on. This lab was full of boxes, and the boxes were full of tins – tins a lot like Scruff's food. I picked up one of them. The label was all scrambled, like my eggs in the morning.

'Scruff, what do I always say? Don't eat things you can't read.'

'DB, this must be what they make in this lab,' exclaimed Sophie. 'It's a Top Secret project so it would be in code!' That kid was a smart one.

AQZHM ONVDQ BZS ENNC

Help Detective Brownie and Sophie crack the code – change each letter to the one after it in the alphabet!

No wonder my pal Scruff was acting up – he'd eaten kitty kibble designed to make cats smarter. I looked around. There were lots of other tins piled up.

'Say Sophie, not all of these tins are the same… I bet they make this food for dogs too We've just got to find the right one!'

'If that code works on one tin, it must work on the others as well!' Sophie said, and started searching the labels.

Which one of these labels says 'BRAIN POWER DOG FOOD'?

A AQZHM ONVDQ ENW ENNC

B AQZHM ONVDQ CNF ENNC

C AQZHM ONVDQ BNV ENNC

tore open the ring pull on the right can.
cruff gave it a suspicious sniff and then ate
s contents down in one. He paused. Sophie
nd I held our breath. Scruff barked and
vagged his tail.

'Nice of you to join us again, Scruff.'

he three of us left the lab and found the
thers, joining in at the back of the group.
r Powell from the university was telling them
bout the special pet food she and her fellow
cientists made. She presented Scruff with a
n of their Brain Power Dog Food. He stared
ard at the label before letting Sophie put it
n her bag. Our Leader was handing out
cience investigator badges. Sophie
oked doubtful.

Do you think we earned those? We didn't go
n the whole tour.' Electrical engineering,
orensics, code-breaking – we sure had
arned those. I patted her on the back.

We came here to solve mysteries and get
adges. And we're all out of mysteries.'

ase solved

Need clues? Turn to page 76.

Join the super crew

Biowoman

From microscopic bacteria to the gigantic blue whale, if it's living then Biowoman wants to know about it. She's got green fingers, a big heart and a fascination with the natural processes of life on Earth. Find her in zoos, on farms, under the sea, in the lab – anywhere things are growing.

Find out what these science superheroes are into – they'll show you where to go.

Humanista

If she looks like she's distracted, she probably is – Humanista's listening to the beat of her own heart. Understanding the body takes a strong stomach, and Humanista is impossible to gross out. She's also keen to explore the limits of the human mind – who knows what's lurking in there…!

Lab Girl

Explosive elements, radioactive materials, bubbling conical flasks and blazing Bunsen burners – these are a few of Lab Girl's favourite things. Her curiosity knows no bounds and she's always got a new experiment on the go. Protective goggles and a lab coat are a must when she's around!

Biowoman's crew

Ecologist, Marine Biologist, Microbiologist

Cultivate your knowledge on pages 24 to 29 and 50 to 55.

Humanista's crew

Doctor, Nutritionist, Psychologist

Stretch yourself with pages 14 to 23.

Lab Girl's crew

Forensic Scientist, Chemist, Toxicologist

Activate some fun on pages 30 to 43.

Illustrated by Emma McCann

The Force

Gravity can really bring you down, right? Well, not The Force – she doesn't see the point of staying stuck on the ground when she could be building a plane and flying! She's always working on a new invention and isn't afraid to take a big step into the invisible unknown.

Mama Earth

No one understands the value of taking things slow like Mama Earth – she's been watching the planet build up its rocky layers since the beginning of time. She knows the secrets of the oceans, mountains, deserts and rainforests. And if she says a volcano is going to blow, you'd better listen!

Space Cadet

She's not really on this planet, but that's no bad thing! Space Cadet can name all the stars in the sky, and plans to move to a different solar system when our technology catches up with her dreams. She's keeping an open mind about alien life forms and is fascinated by black holes.

The Force's crew

Geophysicist, Mechanical Engineer, Particle Physicist

Reach top speed on pages 45 to 49.

Mama's crew

Gemologist, Palaeontologist, Volcanologist

Dive right in to pages 56 to 65.

SC's crew

Aeronautical Engineer, Astronaut, Astrophysicist

Prepare for blast-off with pages 66 to 75.

Top tip

Check out page 76 for a little bit about what each of the superheroes' crew members do. But you could also look the names up online to get the complete low-down on their amazing jobs. And if you're having trouble pronouncing any of them, just ask an adult to help!

Web safe

Magical powers

How do you tell whether something is an apple? You check the colour, feel its smooth skin and round shape, smell its appley smell, hear the crunch as you bite into it and taste that familiar sweetness. To do all this, you're using your five senses of sight, touch, smell, hearing and taste.

But did you know that we actually have more than just these five senses? Our bodies are sensing all sorts of things for us every day without us even realising.

Here are your top five lesser-known magical powers!

You know all about the five senses, right? They help you to understand the world around you. But your body's got more senses up its sleeve than you might think...

1 Magnetic sense

Some scientists believe that those of us with a good sense of direction have taken control of our ability to sense the Earth's magnetic fields. Some people can even tell whether they're facing north or south without a compass! This is the same sense that allows birds to know where they are going when they migrate to different countries.

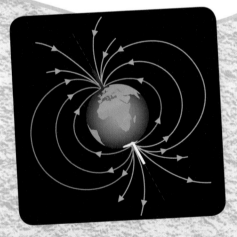

Badge link

Agility

Healthy heart

2 Clockwork sense

Have you ever woken up just before your alarm clock goes off? We have a body clock that is linked to our patterns for sleeping and waking up. We are also able to tell how much time has passed, whether that's an hour or a whole summer. Scientists still don't know how we can do this, but they do know that younger people can do it more easily than older people.

Breathe-easy sense

(3) Special nerve cells in your body monitor the levels of oxygen and carbon dioxide in your blood. Depending on whether they sense that these are low or high, you will automatically increase how much and how deeply you breathe. Your body also lets you know how full your lungs are, so that you don't just keep on breathing in.

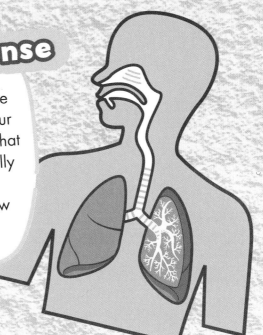

Greedy guts sense

(4) That feeling you get towards the end of a big, yummy meal? You know, the one where you don't think you can eat one more bite? That's yet another sense – your sense of fullness. Special cells tell your brain when your stomach is stretching and becoming full. But the brain can take a while to catch up, so if you eat too quickly you might end up with a stomach ache!

Tightrope walker sense

(5) Stand on one leg. Close your eyes. Now wave your arms in the air. Feel a bit silly? Probably. But if you're still upright then your sense of balance must be great! This is the sense that stops you falling over when you're walking around or standing still, and it's controlled by your inner ear. That's why if you have a very bad cold or ear infection you might feel a bit dizzy or wobbly.

Hidden wonder

Oxygen express

An adult human has between 8 and 10 pints of blood on average. You probably knew that. But did you know that in those 8 to 10 pints are about 20 trillion red blood cells (that's 13 zeros, or 20 million million). There are so many of these clever cells because they have to carry oxygen to every single cell in our body.

Food express

Another job that blood does is take fuel to the rest of the body. This fuel is in the form of glucose (sugar to you and me), which is carried in the plasma fluid part of our blood (salty water). But, this means our blood is so full of good things that it makes us very popular with parasites like mosquitoes, lice and leeches. Eurgh!

Badge link

First aid

Healthy heart

Protection express

Our blood also contains mean little guard dogs called white blood cells – over 40 billion of them. They protect us from things in the outside world that can harm us, like bugs, colds and other infections. Anytime your body feels under attack, it sends white blood cells over to fight the invaders. A single white blood cell will do a patrol of your body once every minute!

Tube network

So just how does blood get around our bodies to do all these amazing things? By taking the tube, of course! Veins, arteries and capillaries are little tubes or tunnels that our blood uses to travel all through our body. And it is quite some tube system – it's about 60,000 miles long. That's long enough to go around the planet twice!

Time to heal

Our blood also helps us heal when we get cuts and scratches. It does this by creating a protective layer over the wound. We call this a scab, and it is made of little things called platelets stuck together with something called protein. The scab works a bit like a plaster – it stops any more blood escaping, as well as not letting in any infections from the outside. So, next time you feel like picking or scratching that scab… Don't!

Scary-tasty brekkie

Want to know what blood looks like under a magnifying glass? Just make this yummy bloody breakfast! Mix 110g Cheerios with red food colouring for red blood cells, add two marshmallows for white blood cells and two big handfuls of blueberries for platelets. Pour in milk or apple juice for plasma and enjoy!

Hallowe'en special

For a trick or treat no one will forget, just mix water, red food colouring, golden syrup, chocolate powder and cornflour together to make gruesome fake blood. Want it thicker? Add more cornflour. Want it runnier? Add more water. Want it darker and spoooooookier? Add more chocolate. Want it bloodier and scarier? Add more food colouring!

Lend a bionic hand

When you move, walk, dance, or jump, you are using bones, joints and muscles.

Joints

Bones are tied to other bones with straps called ligaments, and joints are where two bones meet. Ligaments and joints both make it possible for the different parts of our body to bend. Rubbery stuff in our joints called cartilage protects our bones from rubbing together in our joints.

Bones

Your bones support your body, protect your internal organs (like your brain, heart, lungs and liver) and make you the shape you are.

Muscles

Muscles are attached to our bones with cords called tendons. When you want to move, your brain sends messages down your spinal cord to your muscles. The muscles then tighten (contract) or go floppy (relax) and pull on the tendons, which move your bones. Just think, every time you wiggle, hundreds of little messages are being sent to your muscles!

Badge link

See how it works

Waggle your fingers and watch your tendons move on the back of your hand. Now get going on this mechanical version to see how everything works together. You may need an adult's help as it's quite fiddly!

Be safe

You will need

- Paper
- Pen/pencil
- Scissors
- Paper straws
- Glue
- Wool or string
- Sticky tape

What to do

① Draw around your hand on a piece of paper and carefully cut it out.

② Mark on your paper hand where your knuckles bend (you have three on each finger).

③ Cut a piece of straw for each finger long enough to go from your first knuckle to your finger tip.

④ Mark on each straw where your other knuckles are.

⑤ Make a snip in the straws where you have marked each knuckle. Be careful not to cut through the straw.

⑥ Cut a triangle into the bottom of each straw. Now stick your five straws on to the paper hand.

⑦ Take five more paper straws and cut a triangle at the top of each. Line up the triangles with those at the bottom of each finger so they form diamonds, trim the other ends to fit and stick each straw on the hand to form your 'metacarpal' bones.

⑧ When the glue has dried, thread wool through the straws of each finger all the way to the tip. Use sticky tape to stick the strings to the other side of the finger.

⑨ Now you can pull the strings and see how your bones move!

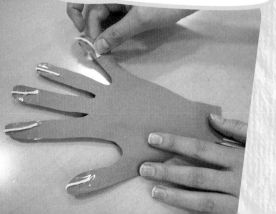

19

London to Rio

The next Olympic and Paralympic Games are taking place this year in Rio de Janeiro, Brazil. For all the athletes taking part it will have been a long and hard road to get there...

Chill, stretch, say 'aah'

Here are some ways top athletes get ready to be their best – which do you fancy?
- Ice baths after each training for faster recovery.
- Massage weekly for aches and pains.
- Stretching to stay flexible.
- Gym work to keep the body strong and prevent injury.
- Mind training to improve focus, motivation and learn how to cope with pressure.
- Tests and health checks to measure the body's performance and spot injury.
- SLEEP – at least eight hours every night to rest tired bodies, but some athletes can sleep up to 14 hours!

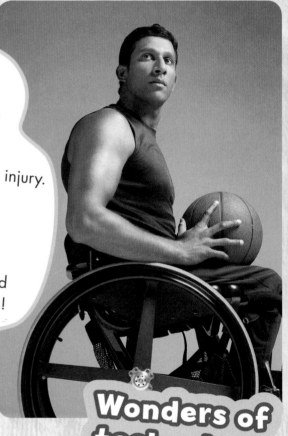

Badge link

Disability awareness

Healthy heart

Sports

Wonders of technology

Many different sports – from cycling and sailing to judo and gymnastics – rely on research and new inventions in order for athletes' performance to continue to improve. This is especially true for Paralympians – London 2012 saw some of the most advanced prosthetic (replacement arms and legs) and wheelchair technology ever. The coaches for the Team GB wheelchair basketball team even use some of the same tech as Formula One! So you shouldn't be surprised that Team GB will be spending a whopping £200,000 on sport science in the run-up to Rio!

Eating for gold

Could you eat like a champion? See if you've got the know-how to fill in the gaps correctly. Answers on page 76.

 1 Breakfasts like ___a___ release energy slowly and help athletes train longer.

a) Porridge, fruit and yoghurt
b) Waffles, bacon and syrup
c) Cereal, milk and a cup of tea

 2 Vitamins in ___b___ help clean up harmful chemical waste produced by the body during heavy exercise.
a) Chocolate and crisps
b) Salad and veg
c) Eggs and soldiers

 3 Protein from ___b___ helps repair muscles and other tissues tired and worn after hard work.
a) Gummy sweets
b) Chicken
c) French cheese

4 The body carries only 90 minutes' worth of fuel for hard exercise. This is called glycogen and is made from carbohydrates like ___c___, which athletes eat lots of to refuel properly.
a) Chips and burger buns
b) Rice cakes and crisp breads
c) Pasta and rice

5 We need LOTS of oxygen to exercise. For this our body needs loads of blood cells to carry oxygen all around our body. Lean ___c___ is a favourite meal for many athletes as it's full of iron, which we need to create more blood cells.
a) Fishfingers
b) Beans
c) Steak

6 Even athletes have a sweet tooth! But bear in mind that they're very good about having the odd naughty treat once every ___c___ at most.
a) Three months
b) Three days
c) Three weeks

The hard yards

Training for Olympic glory in numbers, great and small.
- 6 days a week, 6 hours a day, of training for all (at least!).
- 40 miles an hour average speed by track cyclist Laura Trott.
- 120 miles a week run by runner Mo Farah.
- 5,000 calories a day on average eaten by the Brownlee brothers (equivalent to 32 boiled eggs, 3 kilos of cooked spaghetti or 14 pints of full-fat milk!).
- 6,200 miles a year rowed by GB rowing team.
- 10,000 hours in training by heptathlete Jess Ennis-Hill for London 2012.
- 90,000 metres a week swum by open water champion Keri-Anne Payne.

21

Steeplechase challenge

Your shoelace comes untied. Stand on one leg until your next go

Perfect landing! Do a star jump and move forward 2 spaces

What to do

Grab some friends and decide who is going first by rolling the dice. The highest number goes first. If you land on a square with a forfeit, reward or challenge you must do as it says on the square before the next person takes their turn. If this takes you on to another challenge square then you do not need to do this. If there is someone in your group who may not be able to carry out the forfeits, rewards or challenges, adapt what they have to do so that everyone can be involved!

You collide with a rival. Choose someone to do a forward roll with

Did you know?

Ding
Dong
Ding
Dong

The steeplechase originated in Ireland in the 18th century, with people racing from one church's steeple to another. It's now an Olympic sport, but women have been competing only since 2008.

Badge link

Healthy heart

Sports

You fall at the water jump - go back 3 spaces

You jump too soon! Jump up and down until your next go

Illustrated by John Haller

Start

Oh no! You dipped too early – miss a go

Fastest off the line – move forward 3 spaces

False start – miss a go

You trip at the first jump – go back 1 space

Finish

You will need

- ⊙ Counters
- ⊙ Dice

You land badly and injure your foot. Hop on one foot until your next go

Secret science

Preparing for the 28 hurdle jumps and 7 water jumps in the 3,000m race requires a combination of speed, endurance and mental strength. You must practise to find the best moment for you to leap over the hurdle – too soon or too late will force your body to use too much energy or slow you down. You also need to work out the best angle and positioning of your body as you fly through the air so that you can clear the hurdle, land properly and maintain speed. And you'll need to use some positive thinking to get you through to the end. Phew!

You overtake a competitor - swap positions with another player ahead

First over jump! Have another go

Animal antics

You might not think these animals are cute, but they all have superpowers that are pretty amazing.

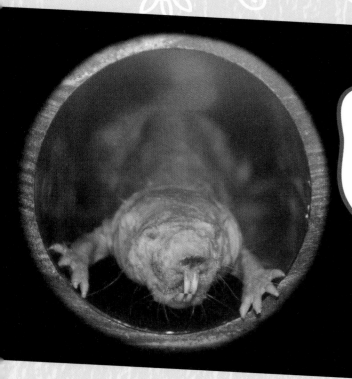

Reverse runners

Naked mole-rats burrow with their mouths. They close their lips behind their teeth so they don't swallow soil. They can also run backwards just as fast as forwards! Can you?

Clever camouflage

The mimic octopus can change its shape and colour to look like a poisonous lionfish, jellyfish or sea snake. It can even make itself look like a sandy rock when it wants to hide.

Badge link

Terrifying tears

If you startle a horned lizard, watch out! They can squirt blood from their eyes up to 1.5m to scare off other animals.

Speedy spitters

Swifts can fly at up to 70mph, and stick their nests on to walls or buildings using their own spit. Yuck!

A dangerous dinner

Cinnabar moth caterpillars eat a poisonous plant called ragwort to make themselves poisonous (and taste nasty) to birds – don't try this at home!

Nosy navigators

Salmon are born in rivers, then swim down to the sea as adults. When it's time for them to breed, they find their way back using their sense of smell, swimming hundreds of miles upstream.

Worms are welcome

Make a worm hotel

See these amazing animals in action!

Worms might be slimy, but they are great for gardens – they break up the soil and turn waste into compost, so plants grow better.

You will need

- Large plastic bottle
- Scissors
- Sticky tape
- Small plastic bottle with lid
- Water
- Soil
- Spoon
- Sand
- 2 or 3 worms
- Dead leaves, vegetable peelings or used teabags
- Black paper

What to do

1. Cut the top off a large plastic water bottle (you may need an adult to help you) and stick tape over any sharp edges.

   Be safe

2. Fill a small plastic bottle with water and screw the lid on tight. This will help keep your worms cool and happy in their hotel.

3. Put a 3cm layer of soil into the large bottle, then stand the small bottle upright inside it.

4. Use the spoon to add a layer of sand around the small bottle.

Badge link

Gardener

Illustrated by Jackie Stafford

(5) Add another layer of soil, then another of sand. Keep going until the large bottle is almost full.

(6) Pour in water a little at a time until the soil and sand are damp but not soggy.

(7) Add your worms and cover with the veggie peelings or leaves. This is their food!

(8) Roll the black paper into a tube just a little bigger than the large bottle and tape into place.

(9) Slide the tube over the bottle. Worms like the dark, so lift it up only a couple of times a day. You should see the layers mixing as your worms burrow through the soil and drag food underground.

(10) After a week, release your worms into a garden or park.

Did you know?

Every year in Cheshire, north-west England, over 100 teams get together for a worm-charming competition. The team that brings the most worms to the surface in half an hour wins a golden worm trophy – and the record is an incredible 567!

Words beneath the waves

Put on your snorkel and dive under the sea for word searches, dingbats and anagrams.

Something fishy going on...

Lots of things that live under the sea are named after something that lives on land. Can you find ten sea animals in the grid?

Sea lion
Parrotfish
Sea horse
Water bear
Sea cow
Dogfish
Water bee
Sea bat
Catfish
Sea slug
Sea snake

One of these is made up and isn't in the grid – which is it?

R	A	E	B	R	E	T	A	W	H
E	H	D	J	U	N	E	M	S	P
W	S	E	A	C	O	W	I	E	R
A	E	S	P	L	O	F	M	A	I
P	A	R	R	O	T	F	I	S	H
E	S	O	S	A	P	P	R	N	E
T	L	H	C	S	E	A	B	A	T
R	U	A	P	E	V	A	W	K	S
C	G	E	N	O	I	L	A	E	S
T	H	S	I	F	G	O	D	N	G

Badge link

Communicator

Illustrated by Sandra Aguilar

Let's go Began Mob Chic *

Solve the anagrams (mixed-up words) to find things you might see on the beach.
*beachcombing

CHITFLUTES
SLOTTEB
AWESEED   FOODWRIT
DATENCLASS   IFLOSS
DUKE BED CATNAPS GRIMEBARS

Struggling? Turn to page 76.

Did you know?

In 1997, millions of pieces of Lego fell into the sea from a ship sailing off the coast of Cornwall in the south-west of England. The pieces (including dragons, flowers and divers) are still being washed up on the beach today!

1.
C C C C C C C

The
3.
C   PoFISHND
2.

4. CALMSTORM

5. SOMETHINGTHISFISHY

6. O C E A N

Say what you sea

Can you find the watery sayings in these clues? Here's the first one to get you started.

SUBMARINE = YELLOW SUBMARINE

29

In your element

What links you, the Indian Ocean, a kangaroo and a chocolate bar? Atoms and elements, of course!

Everything is made up of **atoms** – you, a bus, your school, even your pet! Atoms are so tiny that scientists need a very special microscope to see them. But within a tiny atom are even smaller parts – **protons**, **neutrons** and **electrons**.

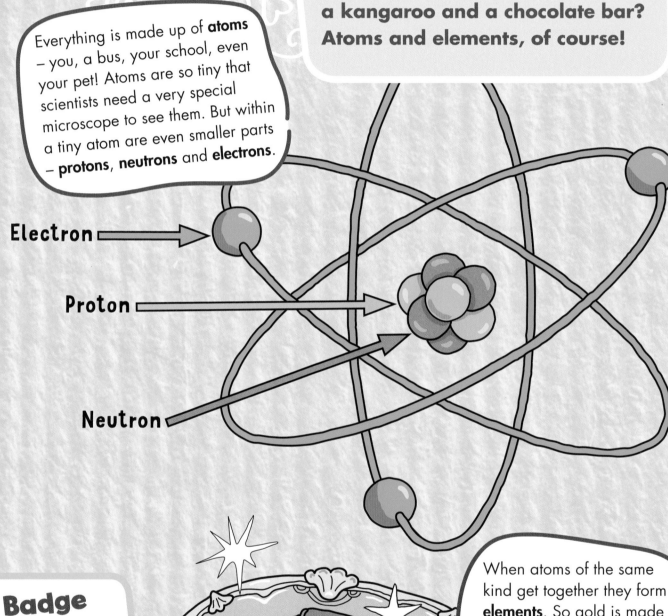

Electron

Proton

Neutron

Badge link

When atoms of the same kind get together they form **elements**. So gold is made up of lots of **gold** atoms, just as mercury is made up of **mercury** atoms and silver of **silver** atoms.

Illustrated by Molly Sage

Look around at your family and friends. They are probably a mix of different heights, sizes and features, right? But did you know that all of you are made up of the same six elements? Nearly 99% of the human body is made up of **oxygen**, **carbon**, **hydrogen**, **nitrogen**, **calcium** and **phosphorus**.

99% the same

And if you think that's amazing, how about this: you are made of stardust! The atoms in our bodies were made in stars many billions of years ago and travelled across space when the stars exploded.

Now you know the names of nine elements. But there are 118 in total, and each one has a symbol and a number.

It's easy to see how some of them got their symbols – oxygen is O and carbon is C. But some of them are very unusual – gold is Au and iron is Fe (they are the short forms of *aurum* and *ferrum*, the Latin words for gold and iron).

The number is the number of protons (remember them? Look at the opposite page again if not!) in the atoms of these elements, so hydrogen is 1, because it has only one proton.

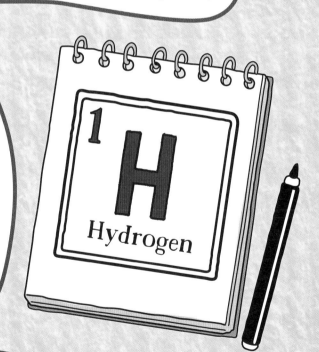

1
H
Hydrogen

If you had 118 books, how would you arrange them on your shelves? You could do it by height or by the name of the author or even by subject. Scientists organise the chemical elements into a chart called the Periodic Table.

It starts with hydrogen, with its atomic number of 1, and goes all the way to 118. Turn the page to check it out...

The Periodic Table

Periods →

Alkali Metals Group 1

Impress your friends by learning the first ten elements by heart and making up a tune to sing them to! Remember to read across the table first, then down, so hydrogen, helium, lithium, beryllium, boron, and so on.

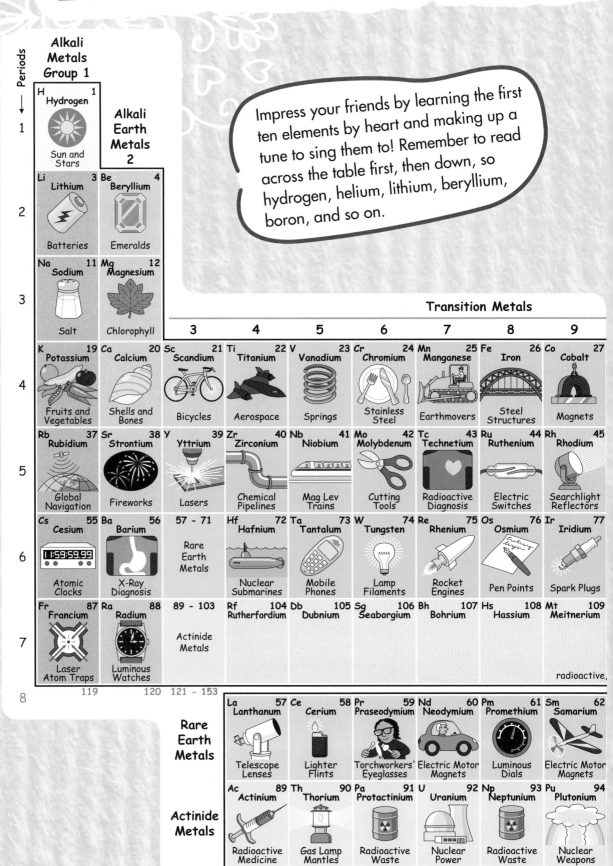

Period 1
- H 1 — Hydrogen — Sun and Stars

Alkali Earth Metals 2

Period 2
- Li 3 — Lithium — Batteries
- Be 4 — Beryllium — Emeralds

Period 3
- Na 11 — Sodium — Salt
- Mg 12 — Magnesium — Chlorophyll

Transition Metals

Groups: 3 4 5 6 7 8 9

Period 4
- K 19 — Potassium — Fruits and Vegetables
- Ca 20 — Calcium — Shells and Bones
- Sc 21 — Scandium — Bicycles
- Ti 22 — Titanium — Aerospace
- V 23 — Vanadium — Springs
- Cr 24 — Chromium — Stainless Steel
- Mn 25 — Manganese — Earthmovers
- Fe 26 — Iron — Steel Structures
- Co 27 — Cobalt — Magnets

Period 5
- Rb 37 — Rubidium — Global Navigation
- Sr 38 — Strontium — Fireworks
- Y 39 — Yttrium — Lasers
- Zr 40 — Zirconium — Chemical Pipelines
- Nb 41 — Niobium — Mag Lev Trains
- Mo 42 — Molybdenum — Cutting Tools
- Tc 43 — Technetium — Radioactive Diagnosis
- Ru 44 — Ruthenium — Electric Switches
- Rh 45 — Rhodium — Searchlight Reflectors

Period 6
- Cs 55 — Cesium — Atomic Clocks
- Ba 56 — Barium — X-Ray Diagnosis
- 57 - 71 — Rare Earth Metals
- Hf 72 — Hafnium — Nuclear Submarines
- Ta 73 — Tantalum — Mobile Phones
- W 74 — Tungsten — Lamp Filaments
- Re 75 — Rhenium — Rocket Engines
- Os 76 — Osmium — Pen Points
- Ir 77 — Iridium — Spark Plugs

Period 7
- Fr 87 — Francium — Laser Atom Traps
- Ra 88 — Radium — Luminous Watches
- 89 - 103 — Actinide Metals
- Rf 104 — Rutherfordium
- Db 105 — Dubnium
- Sg 106 — Seaborgium
- Bh 107 — Bohrium
- Hs 108 — Hassium
- Mt 109 — Meitnerium — radioactive,

Period 8
119   120   121 - 153

Rare Earth Metals
- La 57 — Lanthanum — Telescope Lenses
- Ce 58 — Cerium — Lighter Flints
- Pr 59 — Praseodymium — Torchworkers' Eyeglasses
- Nd 60 — Neodymium — Electric Motor Magnets
- Pm 61 — Promethium — Luminous Dials
- Sm 62 — Samarium — Electric Motor Magnets

Actinide Metals
- Ac 89 — Actinium — Radioactive Medicine
- Th 90 — Thorium — Gas Lamp Mantles
- Pa 91 — Protactinium — Radioactive Waste
- U 92 — Uranium — Nuclear Power
- Np 93 — Neptunium — Radioactive Waste
- Pu 94 — Plutonium — Nuclear Weapons

of the Elements

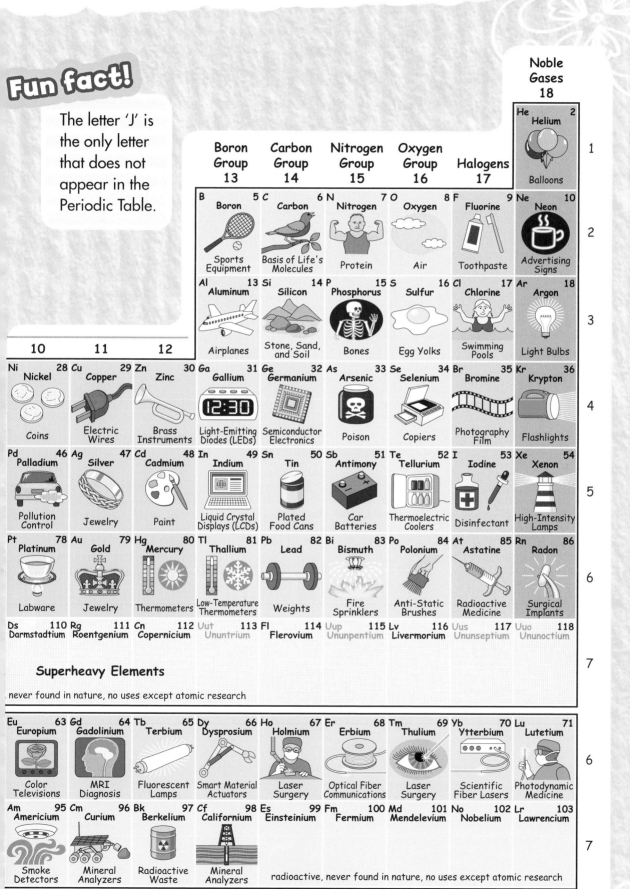

Noble Gases 18

Boron Group 13 — Carbon Group 14 — Nitrogen Group 15 — Oxygen Group 16 — Halogens 17

He Helium 2 — Balloons

B 5 Boron — Sports Equipment
C 6 Carbon — Basis of Life's Molecules
N 7 Nitrogen — Protein
O 8 Oxygen — Air
F 9 Fluorine — Toothpaste
Ne 10 Neon — Advertising Signs

Al 13 Aluminum — Airplanes
Si 14 Silicon — Stone, Sand, and Soil
P 15 Phosphorus — Bones
S 16 Sulfur — Egg Yolks
Cl 17 Chlorine — Swimming Pools
Ar 18 Argon — Light Bulbs

10 — 11 — 12

Ni 28 Nickel — Coins
Cu 29 Copper — Electric Wires
Zn 30 Zinc — Brass Instruments
Ga 31 Gallium — Light-Emitting Diodes (LEDs)
Ge 32 Germanium — Semiconductor Electronics
As 33 Arsenic — Poison
Se 34 Selenium — Copiers
Br 35 Bromine — Photography Film
Kr 36 Krypton — Flashlights

Pd 46 Palladium — Pollution Control
Ag 47 Silver — Jewelry
Cd 48 Cadmium — Paint
In 49 Indium — Liquid Crystal Displays (LCDs)
Sn 50 Tin — Plated Food Cans
Sb 51 Antimony — Car Batteries
Te 52 Tellurium — Thermoelectric Coolers
I 53 Iodine — Disinfectant
Xe 54 Xenon — High-Intensity Lamps

Pt 78 Platinum — Labware
Au 79 Gold — Jewelry
Hg 80 Mercury — Thermometers
Tl 81 Thallium — Low-Temperature Thermometers
Pb 82 Lead — Weights
Bi 83 Bismuth — Fire Sprinklers
Po 84 Polonium — Anti-Static Brushes
At 85 Astatine — Radioactive Medicine
Rn 86 Radon — Surgical Implants

Ds 110 Darmstadtium — Rg 111 Roentgenium — Cn 112 Copernicium — Uut 113 Ununtrium — Fl 114 Flerovium — Uup 115 Ununpentium — Lv 116 Livermorium — Uus 117 Ununseptium — Uuo 118 Ununoctium

Superheavy Elements

never found in nature, no uses except atomic research

Eu 63 Europium — Color Televisions
Gd 64 Gadolinium — MRI Diagnosis
Tb 65 Terbium — Fluorescent Lamps
Dy 66 Dysprosium — Smart Material Actuators
Ho 67 Holmium — Laser Surgery
Er 68 Erbium — Optical Fiber Communications
Tm 69 Thulium — Laser Surgery
Yb 70 Ytterbium — Scientific Fiber Lasers
Lu 71 Lutetium — Photodynamic Medicine

Am 95 Americium — Smoke Detectors
Cm 96 Curium — Mineral Analyzers
Bk 97 Berkelium — Radioactive Waste
Cf 98 Californium — Mineral Analyzers
Es 99 Einsteinium
Fm 100 Fermium
Md 101 Mendelevium
No 102 Nobelium
Lr 103 Lawrencium

radioactive, never found in nature, no uses except atomic research

Crystal garden

Crystals aren't just for jewellery! Everyday ingredients like salt and sugar naturally form crystals, and you can use both to make this cool collage.

Salty scenery

Create your garden backdrop using salt and paint.

You will need

- Paint
- Paint pots
- Water
- Large paintbrush
- Thick paper
- Salt (table or rock salt, or both)
- Tweezers
- Sponge
- Scissors
- Glue stick

What to do

1 Mix up watery paint in three or four different colours.

2 Brush each colour of paint over a whole sheet of thick paper.

3 While it's still wet, sprinkle salt on to the paint. Experiment with different amounts and sizes of salt crystal. You can even pick up large crystals with the tweezers and dip them in water before placing on the paper.

4 Leave the papers to dry, then brush off any loose salt with a dry sponge.

5 Have a look at the different effects you've created. Cut shapes and patterns such as flowers, mountains and clouds.

6 Glue your shapes on to a blank piece of paper to create your garden backdrop then set aside.

Badge link

Artist

Craft

Science investigator

Sweet trees

Now for some crystal greenery to make the garden scene come alive!

You will need

- 120ml hot tap water
- 200g sugar, plus one spoonful
- 2 glass jars
- Spoon
- Green food colouring
- Wooden skewers or lollysticks
- Plate
- 2 clothes pegs

1) Pour the hot water and 200g sugar into one of the jars and stir until the sugar disappears – it might take a couple of minutes. Add a few drops of food colouring.

2) Dip the skewers into the mixture, then place on a plate. Sprinkle with a little more sugar and leave to dry.

3) Divide the sugar water between the two jars. Clip the skewers into the clothes pegs and balance on the rims of the jars, so the sugary end touches the liquid.

4) Leave in a warm place for a few days, until you see sugar crystals forming on the sticks.

5) Add your crystal trees to the salt garden backdrop and admire your work!

Top tip

You could use other colours to make tall flower spikes for example!

Secret science

When the sugar dissolves in the hot water it becomes a liquid mixture, but as the mixture dries the water evaporates, leaving the sugar behind. The sugar molecules gather together and crystallise into solids, fitting together into a repeating pattern that forms unique shapes.

You got slimed!

Discover how to make your very own gooey, sticky slime!

Basic slime

You will need

- 120ml clear PVA glue
- 120ml cold water
- 120ml liquid starch (you'll need an adult's help with this bit – check out the box below for instructions)
- Plastic mixing bowl
- Spoon

What to do

1 Pour the glue into the mixing bowl.

2 Pour the water into the bowl and stir.

3 Add the liquid starch and stir it in. You will see the mixture start to harden. You can mix it with your hands at this point, if you like.

Liquid starch

! Be safe

Grab an adult, plus 125ml water, 5g cornflour, a saucepan, a teaspoon and a mug. Put the cornflour in the mug and mix it with 5ml water. Stir well – the water will turn white. Boil 120ml water in a saucepan. Once boiling, add the cornflour mixture and stir for about 3 minutes. Add more cornflour if too runny. Let the mixture cool.

Badge link

4 Once mixed, your slime is ready! Stretch it, pull it, ooze it between your fingers. You can even try bouncing it!

What next?

With a few extra ingredients you can make your slime truly magical…

Coloured slime

Mix 8 to 12 drops of food colouring into the glue and water before you add the liquid starch.

Glow-in-the-dark slime

Add 40ml of glow-in-the-dark paint to the glue.

Secret science

Slime behaves like a liquid AND a solid, which means it is something called a non-Newtonian fluid (named after Sir Isaac Newton). When you put a straw in water and suck, the water is pulled into the straw. But if you tried to suck the slime up through a straw it would stay firmly put! Basically, it acts like a solid when treated roughly and a liquid when treated gently.

Magnetic slime

Wear rubber gloves for this one! Pour the liquid starch into the bowl first, then add 4 tbsp of iron oxide powder* and stir well. Now add the PVA glue and stir again. Squish it with your hands until it is completely mixed, then pat dry with a paper towel. To play with your magnetic slime you'll need some neodymium (super sensitive) magnets* – be careful as they are extremely strong!

*Ask an adult to help you find this ingredient from an online retailer.

Leave your mark

Guess who?

Fingerprints (sometimes called 'dabs') are an important clue used by the police and detectives. Everyone's fingerprints are different, so if you can match a fingerprint to a person, you know who's been at a crime scene – and so who the guilty person might be!

To find out what your fingerprints look like, press each of your fingertips straight down on an ink pad, or colour in gently with a washable marker pen, and then press them on to this page on the tips of the matching fingers.

Fancy playing at Detective Brownie? It's easy when you know how to dust for fingerprints!

Badge link

It wasn't me!

Do identical twins have the same fingerprints? No, they don't! Every single human being has a different fingerprint – including people with an identical twin. So no, you can't blame your twin sister for the fingerprints on the biscuit tin.

Dust it

Are you a dab hand at fingerprinting? Find out!

You will need

- ◎ Drinking glass
- ◎ Cocoa powder
- ◎ A make-up brush
- ◎ Sticky tape
- ◎ Paper

What to do

1 Press your finger firmly against the outside of the glass so you leave a print.

2 Sprinkle cocoa powder over the print until it's covered.

3 Gently blow away excess powder, or dust it with the make-up brush (be careful not to change the shape of the print).

4 Put a piece of tape over the print (again, be careful not to smudge the print).

5 Peel the tape off the glass very gently.

6 Stick the tape to a piece of paper – the shape of the fingerprint should show up!

Top tip

If the cocoa powder isn't sticking to your fingerprints very well, use a little bit of hand lotion or moisturiser on your fingertip and try again from the start.

How to avoid leaving fingerprints

Can you think of any more clever solutions?

Here are some things you can use if you don't want to leave any fingerprints.

Chopsticks   An oven glove   A litter picker

Did you know?

Fingerprints aren't the only unique shapes in nature. As far as we know, every snowflake has a different shape. It's certainly difficult to prove otherwise – many millions of snowflakes fall per minute around the world, and no one's checking all of them! Tigers also have unique patterns of stripes, which help scientists tell them apart (from a safe distance!).

It's in your DNA

The colour of your eyes, the shape of your nose, whether you're tall or short. These are the things that make you look like you. And they're all down to something called your DNA.

Code for life

So what exactly is DNA? Deoxyribonucleic acid, that's what! A pretty big name for a microscopic molecule. DNA is the material that carries instructions for growth and behaviour. And they are different for every living thing.

Where's my DNA?

In every single cell of your body. Cells are the bricks out of which your body is built, and they use their DNA instruction manuals to make sure they do that job correctly.

Think about you and your best friend – 99.9% of the information in your DNA will be exactly the same. That's why you both look like people, not like cats, or worms, or cacti! But 0.1% is unique to you – that's why you don't look the same. Your mum, dad, siblings and other relatives share some of the 0.1% because you are related. But unless you have an identical twin, scientists would be able to identify the sequences of code in your cells that make you you.

Membrane

Chromatin

Nucleus

Cytoplasm

Badge link

Illustrated by John Hallet

Spit it out!

Catch a glimpse of your own DNA!

You will need

- Plastic bottle
- Surgical spirit (get this from your local chemist or pharmacy)
- Freezer
- 3 drinking glasses
- Water
- 1 tbsp salt
- Washing-up liquid
- Teaspoon
- Light or torch

1 Carefully pour surgical spirit into a plastic bottle and leave it in the freezer for an hour.

 Be safe

2 Half-fill a glass with water and stir in 1 tablespoon of salt.

3 Half-fill another glass with water and this time add a few drops of washing-up liquid.

4 Take a teaspoon of salty water (don't forget which glass is which!) and gargle it around your mouth, then spit into a fresh glass.

5 Now take a teaspoon of the soapy water and add that to the spit mixture.

6 Tilt the glass of spitty, salty, soapy water and slowly pour in the chilled surgical spirit. Stop when the glass is half-full and leave it for another hour. Shine a light through the glass – what can you see? All that cloudy white stuff is your DNA.

 Be safe

Secret science

When you gargled the salt water, you were collecting cells from the inside of your mouth, which ended up in the glass. The detergent in the washing-up liquid breaks down the cells' membranes, releasing everything inside, then the surgical spirit separates the DNA from the rest.

Crime-busters

A person called a forensic scientist compares sources of DNA found at a crime scene in the form of hair, fingernails, skin or saliva to a sample taken from a suspect (usually from their cheeks, like you've just done!) and checks if they are a match. This process isn't 100% accurate, but the chances of finding two people who are not related but have the same DNA code is one in a billion.

Crime scene investigator

Someone has broken into the petting zoo. Use what you've learned about fingerprints and DNA, and follow in the footsteps of Detective Brownie!

To catch the culprit, you need to find:

- 4 fingerprints
- 2 strands of hair
- 1 apple with a bite out of it
- 1 scrap of material (a ripped item of clothing could be a giveaway*)

*This clue is vital. Use it to spot the guilty person!

Illustrated by Beccy Blake

Stuck? Turn to page 77

The zoo keepers have rounded up the bigger animals but they're having trouble finding some of the smaller ones – can you see them hiding anywhere?
- 1 hen
- 4 chicks
- 2 hedgehogs
- 3 rabbits
- 2 kittens
- 3 guinea pigs
- 5 ducks
- 7 mice
- 1 snake

NEW!

Notepad and Pencil
Lined paper, 145x110mm
2202
£1.65

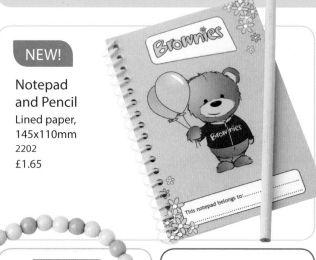

Owl Mug
Height 10.5cm
2199
£3.20

NEW DESIGN!

Bracelet
8305
£2

Owl Hanging Decoration
Length 54cm
2206
£3.75

Teddy*
Height 15cm
2603
£6.50

NEW DESIGN!

Roller Beaker
Height 10cm
8237
£3.75

Owl Lunch Box
18x12.5x6cm
2200
£3.50

Fabric Hairband
2183
£3

Backpack
30x24cm
8701
£10

*Not suitable for children under 36 months

0161 941 2237 to find your nearest volunteer shop or to order from the catalogue

www.girlguidingshop.co.uk to shop online

Wind power

This activity is supported by

 **Rolls-Royce**

to inspire our future scientists and engineers.

Build a miniature wind turbine and then huff and puff to rescue your Lego person.

Badge link

You will need

- Empty 4-pint milk bottle
- Scissors
- Pen or pencil
- Ruler
- Drinking straw
- Staples
- Sticky tape
- Tall beaker or glass
- 2 paperclips
- Water
- String
- Lego person, sticky tack or small rubber (or a Brownie minifig if you have one!)

What to do

1

Carefully cut a 10cm x 10cm square from the plastic milk bottle. You might need an adult's help to get you started.

! Be safe

2

Use a pen or pencil to draw a line between opposite corners so that they cross in the middle.

3

Cut along the lines, starting from the corner, until you reach half-way between the corner and the centre.

45

④

Ask an adult to help you cut a hole in the centre (where the two lines cross), large enough for the straw to fit through. Fold each corner into the centre and staple in place.

⑤ Push the straw through the centre hole. Stick tape over the back of the staples to make the fan's surface smooth and to attach the fan to the straw. This is your turbine.

⑥ Now take your tall beaker or glass and tape two paperclips directly opposite each other on the rim. This is your tower.

⑦ Pour water into the tower so that it is one quarter full and push the straw through the paperclips.

8

Cut a piece of string about 10cm long and stick one end to the middle of the straw. Attach your figure (you could mould a person out of the sticky tack or draw a face on the rubber) to the other end of the string and then drop it into the tower.

9

Now blow hard to turn your wind turbine and save your figure!

Troubleshooting

If you can't lift your figure out of the water, blow harder or make your weight smaller. If your figure doesn't drop back into the water when you aren't blowing, make the weight a little heavier.

Renewable resources

Wind is a renewable energy, which means that we can use as much wind as we want and it never runs out. This is good because other options such as coal are limited and will run out in the future if we keep using them.

Recycling is another good way of reusing something we already have. Once something is no longer required, it can be used for a different purpose. What are you recycling in this activity? What else could you recycle to make your wind turbine? Recycling is great for the environment because it means that fewer resources must be dug from the ground and less is thrown away.

Secret science

In this experiment, your breath acts as the wind. The energy of the wind turns the turbine, and the turning of the turbine turns the straw, rolls up the string and lifts the weight. If there is no wind, the weight will drop again, causing the turbine to turn the other way.

An electrical current is generated by rotating a magnet around a coil of wire. The changing magnetic field causes electricity to flow through the wire. In a wind turbine, the turning of the turbine causes the magnet to turn (instead of the straw in your turbine) and the current to flow. This is how a wind farm works to produce electricity.

Program your friends

Computer code is the language that games, apps and all kinds of other fun things are written in. A computer programmer needs to make sure they tell the computer the right thing to do so everything works properly.

Code course!

Have a go at this activity to get thinking about coding.

You will need

- A large space (like a garden or a large room)
- Obstacles (furniture, boxes or other items)
- Paper
- Pens
- Set of code symbols (see box)
- Friends or family to play with

What to do

1

Set up an obstacle course in your space using different items. For example, a table for people to crawl under, boxes to step in, a hose zigzagged on the ground to follow.

Badge link

Communicator

Computer

48

② Write directions to navigate the course using the code symbols below and any extra information you think is needed (how far to turn, for example). You could add your own symbols if you like.

③ Give your code to a friend or family member. Ask them to read the code out to another friend or family member who has to act like a computer – following the instructions exactly as read out.

④ Do you need to change your code to make it easier to follow? Did anyone get stuck because you told them to step into a box but forgot to tell them to step out of it, for example? If so, update your code and try again.

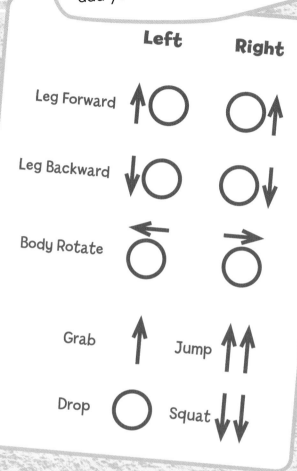

	Left	Right
Leg Forward	↑◯	◯↑
Leg Backward	↓◯	◯↓
Body Rotate	←◯	◯→
Grab	↑	
Jump		↑↑
Drop	◯	
Squat		↓↓

Secret science

When we ask people to do something we rely on shared knowledge and we often don't have to give very detailed instructions. However, when you tell a computer to do something you have to use clear instructions as computers can only follow set rules. Programming involves a lot of logical (or step-by-step) thinking to make sure that the code tells the computer exactly what to do.

Get online and try coding for real!

- pluralsight.com/kids (free online course)
- itunes.apple.com/us/app/daisy-the-dinosaur/id490514278 (iPad app)
- scratch.mit.edu/ (free, used in some schools)
- stencyl.com/ (for creating games)

Web safe

49

Bottled ecosystem

An ecosystem is a community of living things interacting with the place in which they live. This one fits in a bottle!

What to do

1 Take the labels off the plastic bottles. Carefully cut the top off one bottle (keep this) and the bottom off the other.

You will need

- 2 two-litre clear plastic bottles
- Scissors
- Pair of old flesh-coloured tights
- Rubber band
- Gravel
- Potting soil
- Plant seeds (mustard, cress or grass)
- A few dead leaves and small sticks
- 1 or 2 worms and/or beetles
- Aquarium gravel
- Distilled water
- Scoop of algae
- Pond weed or other aquatic plants
- 1 or 2 guppies and/or water snails
- Clear sticky tape

2 Take the bottle with the bottom cut off and remove the cap. Cut a section from a pair of tights, cover the bottle neck and fix in place with a rubber band.

3 Turn the bottle upside down. Add 3cm of gravel, then 6cm of soil.

Badge link

Top tip

Ask an adult to help you get hold of all the things you need from your local garden centre or pet shop. Or for a similar but slightly easier activity, try the worm hotel on pages 26 to 27.

50

Illustrated by Esther van den Berg

4) Plant your seeds, then pop in some dead leaves and small sticks, and introduce your worms or beetles to their new home. Put your earth environment safely to one side.

5) Take the bottle that you cut the top off and line the bottom with 3cm of aquarium gravel. Pour in distilled water until the bottle is half full. Add your scoop of algae, the pond weed or other aquatic plants and your new water pets.

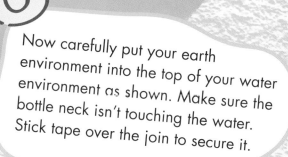

6) Now carefully put your earth environment into the top of your water environment as shown. Make sure the bottle neck isn't touching the water. Stick tape over the join to secure it.

7) Finally, take the bottle top that you cut off in step 1 and attach to the top of your bottled ecosystem with sticky tape.

8) Pop on a sunny window ledge and watch your ecosystem flourish!

Secret science

Each item in your ecosystem has a role to play in keeping all the other things alive. Sunshine kickstarts the cycle of life, making the water evaporate, condense in the top of the bottle and water the seeds. The plant grows and uses the sun's energy to produce oxygen for your creatures to breathe in, while absorbing the carbon dioxide they breathe out. The dead leaves and algae provide food and nutrients.

Seriously wild snacks

Whether you're on a nature walk, in your garden, or about to start Guides and go camping for the first time, there are some amazing (and surprisingly tasty) plants all around you.

Delicious dandelions

Dandelion leaves aren't just for rabbits – they make a tasty salad leaf, and can also be steamed like spinach or added to a stir-fry or soup. The flowers' bright yellow petals can be eaten too, as well as made into wine. And the roots can be dried and roasted to use as a coffee substitute for those who are feeling very adventurous!

Did you know?

Dandelion seeds can travel an amazing five miles from the plant, so no wonder so many gardens are full of this yummy weed!

Brilliant blackberries

Look out for these juicy fruits in your local park or green space. They're in season from late August to October, and just one handful of berries counts as one of your five a day. Expect to feel great after eating them as well – they're full of healthy things called antioxidants, low in sugar and high in vitamin C. But watch out for prickly brambles and always remember to wash them well before eating!

Be safe

Badge link

Cook

Gardener

Make a simple blackberry sauce

You'll need 250g blackberries, 100ml water and 50g sugar. Bring all the ingredients to a boil then simmer for five minutes. Strain your sauce through a sieve and pour on top of yoghurt or ice cream. Mmmm!

Very tasty violets

Small and purple, these flowers are often found in shady spots. They can be eaten raw, made into jelly or even cooked into a porridge. But the prettiest way to eat violets is to crystallise them by brushing them with beaten egg white then covering with sugar. Sprinkle them on top of your favourite cake or dessert. You can do this with other flowers too, such as roses, lavender and primroses.

Did you know?

Throughout history, violets have been used in medicines, perfumes, make-up, clothes dyes and paint.

Nommy nasturtiums

These bright orange flowers are easy to grow at home, and taste slightly sweet and peppery. The plant's common name actually comes from the Latin *nasus tortus* meaning screwed-up nose, which was the face people made when they ate these spicy little things. You could sprinkle the chopped flowers on anything from salads and soups to sandwiches to add a bit of colour and zing!

Make a zesty nasturtium vinegar

You'll need a sealable bottle, nasturtium flowers and white wine vinegar (five flowers per cup of vinegar). Put the flowers in the bottle. Heat up the vinegar to just below boiling, then pour into the bottle as well. Leave to cool and settle. Strain out the flowers and replace with fresh ones.

Be safe

Top tips

- Before you eat any plants you've found or grown outdoors make sure you've checked with an adult first and then washed them thoroughly.
- If you're not totally sure what plant it is – don't eat it. Never eat flowers, plants or berries unless you're certain that they are edible.
- For the best colour and flavour, make sure you get outside to forage on a dry morning before the sun gets too hot, and pick only young flowers and those still in bud.
- Your wild food finds won't stay fresh and tasty for long, so use them that day if possible or pop them in the fridge inside a plastic bag for use over the next couple of days.

Seed sensation

Seeds aren't just for growing – or munching! Try this fun craft to turn simple seeds into a work of art.

You will need

- Old newspapers
- Painting apron
- Poster paints in different colours
- A few small plastic food bags
- Bag of seeds, such as pumpkin or sunflower seeds
- Greaseproof paper
- Glitter (optional)
- Small cardboard box or photo frame
- PVA glue
- Brush or glue spreader
- Sequins, beads or jewels (optional)

What to do

① Spread some newspaper over your table and pop your apron on. Choose your first colour of paint and squirt a small amount carefully into one of the plastic bags. (You don't need much!)

② Pour some seeds into the bag of paint. Holding the bag closed at the top, carefully rub and squish the bag so all the seeds get covered with paint.

Badge link

54

③ Tip the seeds out on to a piece of greaseproof paper. Carefully spread them out to dry. If you want them sparkly, you could sprinkle on some glitter.

④ Now do steps 1 to 3 again with other paint colours. When you have finished, leave your colourful seeds to dry.

⑤ So now you are ready to get decorating! Spread glue over your box or frame, and arrange your seeds in a cool design or pattern. Try to cover all of your box or frame without leaving gaps. If you want to add some sequins, beads or craft jewels, go ahead!

⑥ When it is dry, paint another layer of glue over the top to protect your seeds.

Did you know?

- Seeds contain all the material needed to grow a new plant, hidden inside a protective shell.
- Plants have developed lots of different ways of spreading their seeds. Some, like dandelions, can fly (check out page 52 for more cool facts about this plant)! Other plants hide their seeds in delicious fruits that are eaten by animals or people – such as tomatoes. Some plants even have exploding seed pods!
- The biggest seed in the world is the double coconut or coco-de-mer. It can measure up to 30cm in length.

55

Bedazzled

We all know what diamonds are: sparkly stones that we see in rings and other jewellery. But there is more to them than meets the eye...

What is a diamond?

Diamonds are the hardest substance known to us, and can be cut or scratched only by another diamond. Although we may think of diamonds as being clear, most are actually brown or yellow. But they can come in all colours, and some, such as the bright pink or blue ones, are very rare and valuable.

Where do diamonds come from?

The Earth is made from many different layers, like the layers of skin on an onion. If you dug a hole at least 30 miles deep you could see down to a layer called the mantle. Don't jump down the hole though – the mantle is made of rocks so hot they have melted. And the pressure (that uncomfortable feeling you get in your ears when you dive underwater) would squash you flat! But these conditions are perfect for diamonds to form.

💎 Diamonds are hard but not tough: if you hit one with a hammer you could smash it.

What are diamonds made from?

Diamonds are made from an atom called carbon – the same stuff that makes coal and the graphite in the middle of your pencil. The heat and pressure inside the Earth squeeze the carbon atoms together in a way that creates diamonds instead of pencil leads.

Badge link

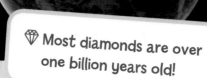

💎 Most diamonds are over one billion years old!

💎 Tiny diamonds have also been found in meteorites, rocks that have travelled from outer space and crashed into Earth.

How do we get diamonds?

We can't go down into the mantle to fetch diamonds – so we have to find the ones that have come out by themselves. Sometimes there will be a huge explosion in the mantle, like a volcano (turn the page for more about these) deep underground, and boiling hot rocks will come shooting up to the surface of the Earth. The rocks cool down and become solid, with diamonds hidden in them. Over time, the rocks wear away and the diamonds can be found. Some may be lying on the ground or in rivers, but most will still be underground. Huge diamond mines are dug to find all the stones.

💎 There are diamond mines in Australia, Brazil, Canada, India and Russia, but around half of the world's diamonds are found in Africa.

💎 Diamonds can also be created in science labs - but experts can tell the difference between 'real' diamonds and human-made ones.

What happens next?

When diamonds come out of the ground they aren't sparkly – they look like dull crystals or the blobs of smooth glass you find on the beach. Diamonds that are chosen to be made into jewellery are cut and polished into shapes that show off their beauty. However, about four fifths of diamonds are not good enough to become jewels. Instead, because of their hardness, these diamonds are useful for making tools such as cutting blades and drills.

💎 The Koh-i-Noor (which means 'Mountain of light') is owned by The Queen and can be seen in the Tower of London. It is one of the most valuable diamonds in the world.

💎 The largest cut diamond in the world is a brown stone called the Golden Jubilee. Found in 1985, it is part of the Crown Jewels of Thailand.

💎 The Hope Diamond is supposed to bring bad luck to anyone who wears it - but actually the stories of a curse were made up by a jeweller who wanted the stone to seem more mysterious!

WARNING: Lava-ruption!

Prepare to get very messy with a home-made volcano lava eruption. Ask an adult first!

You will need

- Clear outside space
- Lots of raked leaves, loose earth or sand
- 500ml bottle of diet cola
- Pack of white, powdery sugar-free mints

What to do

1 Find somewhere clear outside (a large garden or beach is ideal), far away from anything and anyone, and create a little volcano with leaves, earth or sand.

2 Bury your bottle of diet cola in the middle of the volcano, nice and firm, with just the lid sticking out.

3 Unscrew the lid.

Badge link

science investigator

Illustrated by Molly Sag

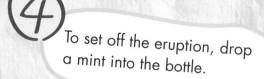

④ To set off the eruption, drop a mint into the bottle.

⑤ Get well away and watch from a distance!

Secret science

Volcanic eruptions happen when the Earth's plates (which are a bit like jigsaw puzzle pieces and fit together to form the Earth's surface) crash into each other. When this happens they squeeze boiling liquid rock out of volcanoes (like ketchup out of a bottle!). Volcano eruptions are VERY dangerous, but they also do our planet some good. This is because the Earth is a bit like a boiling kettle. When steam escapes it releases pressure inside the kettle, which is what is happening during a volcano eruption.

Take it further

Try other fizzy drinks like regular cola, lemonade and fizzy water to see which gives the best fizz eruption. Record your experiments on film or through photos.

Lava, magma and other melting hot facts

- There are over 1,500 LIVE volcanoes around the world.
- Superhot liquid rock inside volcanoes is called magma.
- Superhot liquid rock escaping volcanoes is called lava!
- Volcano scientists – people who study volcanos – are called volcanologists. The most famous were French wife and husband team Katia and Maurice Krafft who visited HUNDREDS of volcanos in their lifetime. They saved thousands of lives over the years by warning people early whenever a volcano was about to erupt. Sadly, they died during an eruption of a volcano they were visiting in Japan in 1991.

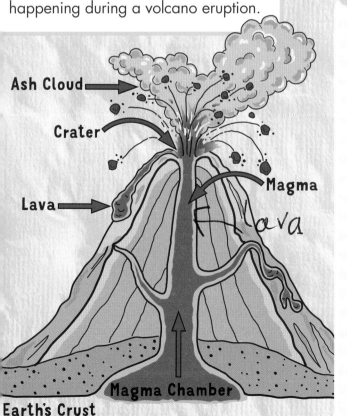

Ash Cloud

Crater

Lava

Magma

Lava

Magma Chamber

Earth's Crust

DANGER: Earthquake!

You will need

- Hole puncher
- 2 cardboard rectangles
- String
- Sticky tape
- A large sheet of newspaper
- Soil or dirt

Get outside and move (teeny tiny) mountains with this easy earthquake activity.

What to do

1 Punch two holes on one side of each cardboard rectangle.

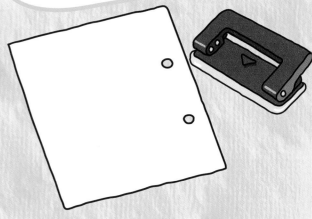

2 Tie a piece of string through the holes on one piece of cardboard, so that you have a loop to hold on to.

3 Do the same to the other piece of cardboard.

Badge link

4 Tape the two pieces of cardboard together, down the middle, leaving a little room so they can sit apart.

Illustrated by Molly Sag

⑥ Gently pull on the strings. You will notice that the boards shake as you do this and the earth on top of them moves around.

⑤ Lay the cardboard pieces on top of the newspaper and cover them with dirt.

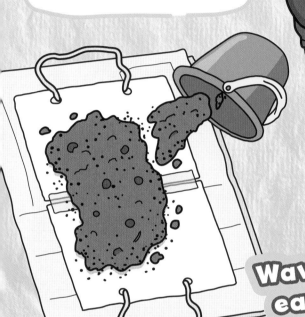

Waves, Richter and other earth-shattering facts

- Every year scientific instruments detect about 500,000 earthquakes around the world.
- Scientists use the different speeds of seismic waves to pinpoint where an earthquake started. This is called the epicentre.
- Scientists measure the strength of an earthquake using something called a 'seismometer' and chart it on the 'Richter scale'.
- The higher the number on the Richter scale, the larger the earthquake. You probably wouldn't even notice a number 3, but a 6 could damage houses if they're not well built.
- The strongest recorded earthquake was in 1960, in Chile – 9.5 on the Richter scale!

Secret science

The wobbling of the boards is a bit like the waves of energy that roll through the Earth during an earthquake. The Earth's crust is made up of huge pieces of flat rock called tectonic plates (the cardboard sheets). As the plates slowly move and rub together, the movement causes seismic (said 'size-mick') waves that travel through the earth to the surface, making it shake and quake.

Dinosums

You'll need to use all your number knowledge (and a calculator if you're desperate) to escape from T-Rex.

Secret sequence

The Fibonacci ('fib-on-archie') sequence is a list of numbers, each made by adding the two numbers before.
So it starts with 1, then 0+ 1 = 1...

2,   3,   5,   8...
(1+1)   (1+2)   (2+3)   (3+5)

Follow the sequence through the grid to escape the ravenous dinosaurs – but be careful, there's only one way out!

START	1	1	4	23	34	76	93
12	4	2	6	17	46	80	108
8	5	3	9	21	67	121	163
13	7	10	25	24	35	76	224
21	34	55	89	72	175	49	325	→ Finish C
43	76	110	144	100	230	152	647
56	64	134	233	377	610	735	326
80	120	237	476	501	987	863	632

Finish A

Finish B

Bones and bits

Had enough? Turn to page 77

Each piece of these dinosaur skeletons has a secret number.

CLAW + TOOTH = 5

TOOTH + TOOTH = 2

BONE + BONE + CLAW = 8

Can you crack the code and solve the sums?
1. CLAW + BONE + BONE + TOOTH = ?
2. TOOTH + ? + CLAW = 7
3. BONE x ? = 8
4. CLAW – TOOTH = ?
5. CLAW + TOOTH + TOOTH = BONE + BONE + ?

Hid in the grid

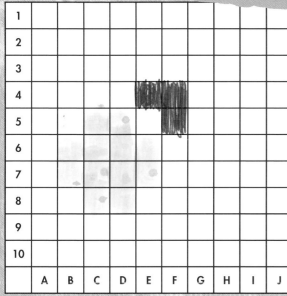

	A	B	C	D	E	F	G	H	I	J
1										
2										
3										
4										
5										
6										
7										
8										
9										
10										

Phew – it looks like you've escaped!
But what's that hurtling through the sky?

Colour in yellow
B5, C4, D4, E3, E5, E8, F3, F6, F7, G2, G3, G4, G5, H2, H3, I1

Colour in brown
B6, B7, C5, C6, C7, C8, D5, D6, D7, D8, E6, E7

Colour in red
E4, F4, F5

Everything else: colour like the sky.

Expert escape

Quick, into one of these caves! But only one of them is safe – use the clues to find the right one.

- The number is more than the number of letters in the word PTERODACTYL.
- If you write the number out as a word, it includes a W and a Y.
- The two digits in it are not the same.
- It is not an odd number.
- It doesn't end in a 0 or a 5.
- If you add the two digits together, you get 6.

Illustrated by Sandra Aguilar

Fossil footprints

You might have seen bones and teeth that are preserved as fossils – but we can also find the tracks and footprints of animals that lived millions of years ago. Make your own, and challenge someone else to uncover them!

You will need

- 300g flour
- 250g salt
- Large bowl
- Wooden spoon
- 240ml hot tap water
- Old tray or plate
- Objects to make imprints with (toy cars and animals, keys, coins, jewellery, buttons - anything with an interesting shape)
- Sand or compost
- Old paintbrush

What to do

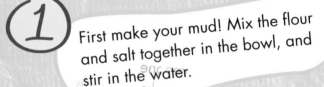

(1) First make your mud! Mix the flour and salt together in the bowl, and stir in the water.

(2) Use your hands to smush the mixture together until it forms a dough.

(3) Squash a thin, even layer of dough on to the plate or tray and leave for one to two hours to dry out a bit.

Badge link

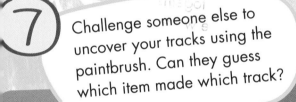

(4) Once the surface is no longer sticky to touch, press the toys and other items into the mud to make imprints. Remember to take them out again!

(5) Leave the plate somewhere safe for 48 hours for the mud to set.

(6) Now cover your 'fossil footprints' in compost or sand. Real fossils are covered and lost for millions of years, but you don't have to wait that long!

(7) Challenge someone else to uncover your tracks using the paintbrush. Can they guess which item made which track?

Secret science

A fossil is like a message in a bottle from the past. In some cases, whole plants, animals and even people have been found captured in tree resin (amber), tar pits and peat bogs, and ice. In others, hard substances such as shell and bone are gradually covered by layers of mud, sand and rock, and over time replaced by minerals to form replicas of what was left behind. Footprints, like the imprints you have just made, are formed in a similar way – they disappear under more layers of mud, which hardens into rock, forming a cast.

Fossil facts

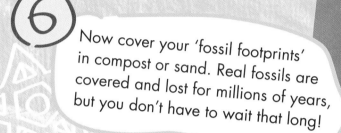

- The term 'fossil' comes from the Latin *fossilis*, meaning 'dug up or out of the earth'.
- The older the rock you're digging through, the older the fossils you will find in it!

Let's do the timewarp

Facts about time that will bend your brain.

We live in the past

About 0.08 seconds (or 80 milliseconds) to be precise. Scientists calculate that this is how long your brain takes to 'compute' reality through your senses and into your conscious mind.

The universe in a year

1 January – the Big Bang creates the universe
31 August – the sun appears
16 September – the Earth appears
21 September – life on Earth appears
25 December – dinosaurs appear!
29 December – dinos rule the planet. Roarsome!
30 December – dinos disappear.
31 December 22:24 – humans appear! How late to the party were we?!

Time slows down

Everyone thinks that time is constant, meaning that it always moves at the same speed. But it doesn't! A brilliant scientist named Albert Einstein came up with a very famous theory that time can move at different speeds. Lots of experiments later proved that he was right, because it's actually the speed of light, and not time, that never changes.

Badge link

Women rock age!

Did you know that, right now, the ten oldest people in the world are all female? Misao Okawa from Japan is the oldest, and was 117 years old in 2015. This means that when she was born we still hadn't invented many, many awesome things like aeroplanes, vacuum cleaners, tea bags, plastic, talking cinema, antibiotics, microwaves, computers, the internet – and the frisbee!

People, people everywhere

It took over a thousand years for the UK's population to double from one million to two million (from about the first to the 12th century). The UK population today of about 64 million is likely to double to over 130 million in just a hundred years! This is because thanks to great advances in medicine, science and technology (and peace!), people live much longer today than ever before.

Pyramids and woolly mammoths

When people think of the Ice Age, most think of woolly mammoths (really big, really hairy cousins of the elephant). But these guys were actually still alive when the pyramids of Egypt were first built – the last known woolly mammoths lived near the North Pole just 4,000 years ago, and the first pyramids were built about 4,600 years ago. Amazingly, these creatures could return! Scientists have just discovered how to combine woolly mammoth DNA with elephant DNA so maybe…

To the skies, moon, stars and beyond

Humans first took to the skies in an aeroplane in 1903. A mere 66 years later in 1969 we landed a human on the moon. And just seven years after that in 1976 we landed a spacecraft on Mars!

Immortal jellyfish

There is a Mediterranean species of jellyfish called *Turritopsis dohrnii* that never dies! It does this by 'recycling' itself over and over and over again from its adult form back to its polyp form (a bit like our baby stage).

Brownies in space!

Once upon a time, many years in the future...

To: StellaInSpace@iss.org
From: Mira@brownies.org.uk

Dear Auntie Stella,
I hope you are well. Some of my friends and I are doing our Science investigator badge at Brownies, and we have to visit a science centre or talk to a scientist about what they do. Please can we come and see you at work?
Love,
Mira x

From: StellaInSpace@iss.org
To: Mira@brownies.org.uk

Hi Mira,
Great to hear from you. I'd love to see you and your friends, and show you around this place. Be ready to leave at 8am on Saturday. Don't worry about a packed lunch, but could you bring some fresh fruit to share?
See you soon!
Auntie Stella x

'Wow!' said Mira as she gazed up at the tall, sleek rocket on the launchpad.
'It's huge!' exclaimed Danika.
'Are we really going in that?' asked Seren, nervously.
'Yes we are, come on!' Mira ran ahead and led the Brownies up a ladder, through a hatch and into the rocket. 'I'm sitting at the front!'
'Seatbelts on, everyone,' called Sally, the Brownies' Leader.
'That's right,' added an astronaut, popping her head in through a door 'Hi guys, I'm Astrid and I'll be your pilot on today's mission to the International Space Station. Now, let's get you all strapped in. And here are some earplugs for you – things will get noisy for a while when we launch.'

Illustrated by Emma McCann

With the Brownies and Sally all safely in their seats and ready to go, Astrid fired up the rockets' thrusters. A roar of sound became louder and louder, and the rocket started to shake. Even Mira wondered for a moment if this was such a great idea. But then she was squashed back into her seat as the rocket lifted off, and she forgot all about her fear in the excitement of blasting into space for the very first time.

About ten minutes later, the Brownies heard Astrid's voice over the intercom.
'All OK back there? We are now in orbit around the Earth and heading for the space station. Any questions?'
'How fast are we going?' called Mira.
'Oh, about 17,500 miles an hour,' replied Astrid. 'We need to go that fast in order to stay in orbit. If we slowed down too much we'd fall back down to Earth.'
'Awesome!' sighed the Brownies.

The rocket ride was over all too quickly, but when the Brownies felt the gentle bumps that meant the rocket was docking with the space station, they became even more excited. Mira was the first to undo her seatbelt.
'I'm flying!' she yelled as she floated around the rocket cabin. It felt amazing, even better than being in the swimming pool. 'Look at this!' She turned a cartwheel in mid-air, but couldn't stop - cartwheeling all the way down the cabin and crashing into the back wall.
'Take it steady,' laughed Sally, but by now all the Brownies were racing round the cabin, bouncing off the walls and ceiling. Being weightless was the best, especially when Astrid came in and showed them some cool zero-gravity dance moves.
A hissing sound meant the airlock was opening, and a

moment later the Brownies floated through it to get their first look inside the International Space Station.

'It's like a submarine,' said Danika.

'It's like a science lab,' said Seren.

'It's like… a spaceship!' breathed Mira in amazement.

'Well, there's a reason for that!' said an astronaut, laughing.

'Auntie Stella!' cried Mira. 'Thanks for having us to visit!'

'It's good to see you all,' replied Stella. 'Do you want to do some exploring?'

'Yes!' the Brownies shouted.

'OK. This is my bedroom. What do you think?'

'That's not a room!' exclaimed Mira. 'It's like a cupboard! How could you sleep in there?'

'See my sleeping bag? It's fixed to the wall so I don't drift away in the night. There isn't much room, but there's enough space for me to relax and read or use my computer. Do you think you could live in there for six months?'

'No way.' The Brownies all shook their heads.

'Well, maybe the bathroom will change your minds. Here it is,' said Stella.

'Where? That's just a pack of wet wipes,' said Danika.

'Yep! That's how we wash in space. Can you imagine trying to have a shower or a bath with all the water floating around? Now, who's brave enough to try the zero gravity loo…?'

The Brownies took a look, but when Stella explained how the toilet worked, with air to suck everything away instead of water to flush it, they decided that no one really needed to go.

'So what do you do all day, Stella?' asked Sally.

'We spend a lot of time looking after the space station. We're a long way from home here, so if anything wears out or goes wrong we need to fix it ourselves. We also have to look after our own bodies. Being weightless for a long time makes our muscles and bones weak, so we spend several hours a day exercising to keep us strong and healthy. And then there's our real work…'

Stella led the Brownies along a tunnel and into an amazing science lab.

'Hello!' Another astronaut greeted them. 'I'm Yuri. I've got loads of experiments on the go. At the moment I'm studying how different materials burn in zero gravity. Look at this.'

The Brownies floated round Yuri and watched as he lit a candle. To their surprise, the flame did not grow into a normal pointy shape but burned small and round, like a blue glowing ball.

'Wow!' they all said.

'Cool, isn't it?' said Yuri. 'And look how water behaves.' He squirted some water into the room and laughed as the Brownies chased the round, wobbly droplets through the air.

'Thanks Yuri,' they all called as they waved goodbye so that Stella could lead them back to the main module for lunch. She added hot water to stuff that looked like rabbit food, but it turned out to be pasta Bolognese and was actually quite tasty. Drinks came in plastic pouches with straws. The Brownies got out the fruit they had brought, and all the astronauts came crowding in to share it.

'This is a treat,' explained Stella. 'We get fresh fruit only when ships come from Earth. Most of the time our food is dried or frozen. Thanks, Brownies!'

When they had finished, Stella took the Brownies for one final surprise. They floated into a small module with a dome-shaped roof made from seven windows. Outside, the huge blue and green Earth slowly turned, with white clouds making patterns over the seas and land. As they watched, the sun disappeared behind the Earth and darkness spread below them. Now all they could see were clusters of tiny golden lights, which Stella explained were the biggest cities. But all around them the darkness of space sparkled with stars.

'It's so beautiful,' sighed Seren. 'Now I understand why you want to live up here. I wouldn't like the bedrooms or the weird toilet but I would love to look at this every day!'

'You're right,' smiled Stella. 'We all feel so lucky to be here. Being an astronaut isn't the most comfortable life, but the chance to see these amazing sights and do all the exciting science work makes it worthwhile. So, do you girls think you'd like to do my job?'

Mira shook her head. 'No way. I'm going to do Astrid's job – flying the rocket. That was awesome!'

Competition time!

Send us your snaps and you could win a selection of Brownie goodies!

One of the best things about being a Brownie is getting to try new things and visit new places – everything is an adventure. It'll be a little while until you can just hop in a rocket and travel into space, but there are still plenty of opportunities for exploration here on Earth.

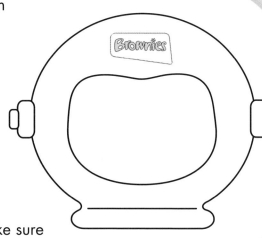

For a chance to win this great prize, all you need to do is send us a photo of you exploring somewhere or something new. What you're doing and who you're with is up to you. But you will need to be wearing something suitable for the task... So we've designed you a special Brownie space helmet! Download it from **www.girlguiding.org.uk/brownies**, colour it in and make sure you're wearing it in your photo.

Send your competition entry (with your name, age and address, as well as your unit's name) by 29 February 2016 via email to **brownieannual@girlguiding.org.uk** or by post to:

Brownie Annual 2016 competition
Girlguiding
17-19 Buckingham Palace Road
London SW1W 0PT

TERMS & CONDITIONS

Entries must be received no later than 29 February 2016.
The winning Brownie will be notified on or before 31 March 2016.
Entries will be judged on creativity, effort and individuality.
The judges' overall decision is final.

Astro-grub

Mira and her Brownie unit got to try some space food when they visited Aunt Stella – pasta Bolognese! But astronauts haven't always been able to eat a dinner as tasty as that...

1961

Yuri Gagarin is the first human in space. He orbits the Earth for just 108 minutes but still manages to eat a meal while he's up there – puréed meat washed down with some chocolate sauce, both stored in toothpaste-style tubes so that he can squeeze them straight into his mouth.

1963

The crews of the Mercury missions still chow down on tubes, but they also have freeze-dried meals that are cooked, quickly frozen and then heated in a vacuum to remove all moisture. The only liquid comes from saliva, so it's not a very pleasant experience! They also eat dehydrated (dried) food in bite-sized cubes coated in jelly to avoid crumbs. It could mean disaster if food particles float away and end up inside any of the hi-tech controls!

1965

By the time Gemini 3 blasts off, tubes have been ditched and freeze-dried foods are now cleverly packaged so astronauts can mix in water – only cold though! There's also more choice, though that doesn't stop Command Pilot Gus Grissom eating a sneaky corned-beef sandwich smuggled up from Earth, landing him in a lot of trouble.

1968

The Apollo 8 spacecraft has both hot and cold water, so astronauts can finally enjoy a hot, tasty meal. And on Christmas Eve, the crew open up their dinner packets to find real turkey. The meat has been through a heating process called thermostabilization, which means it can be stored at room temperature and not go bad. It even comes with gravy and cranberry sauce – what a treat!

1973

The US launches its first space station, a long-term base for astronauts. Skylab has a refrigerator and freezer, meaning fresh foods can be easily stored and the crew can even enjoy some ice cream! Meals can now be heated inside their plastic packets or aluminium cans, and there's a whole galley for preparing and eating dinner, complete with foot-holds to stop people floating around.

Did you know?

Canadian astronaut Chris Hadfield tweeted that when you're in zero gravity, gas and liquid float together in your stomach, meaning you can't burp. So there's only one way for that gas to come out…!

Happy Birthday, Tim!

Sometimes NASA sends a cake up to the space station when it is an astronaut's birthday. Tim Peake (see '2015' box far right) was born on 7 April 1972. If you could design a cake for Tim's 44th birthday in space, what would it look like? Draw a picture. Make sure you use some of the facts you've learned about food in space when you design it!

1991

Helen Sharman becomes the first Briton in space. Girl power! Before she arrived at the International Space Station (ISS), Helen was a chemist for chocolate company Mars, so it's just as well that space food is pretty good by this point. Each astronaut's meal plan is designed for them by special scientists called nutritionists to make sure they get all the nutrients they need.

Illustrated by Rémy Simard

2001

Pizza Hut delivers to space! The US restaurant chain pays a cool $1 million for the publicity stunt, which sees a pizza travel on a Russian spaceship to the ISS, where it is eaten by cosmonaut Yuri Usachov. What would have been your choice of takeaway?

2015

All things going as planned, Brit Tim Peake travels to the ISS in November to spend six months carrying out scientific experiments. If you're reading this while he's out there, he could be enjoying a steak or a sticky toffee pudding right now! But he isn't able to eat whatever he wants, whenever he wants – the space station can store only a certain number of things and there's a set 16-day menu cycle. Tim is allowed two cases of his favourite snacks – though only things that last a long time.

Intergalactic midnight feast

Make a starry night light and then use your imagination.

You will need

- Clean glass jam jar
- Glow-in-the-dark paints
- Paintbrush

What to do

Use the paintbrush to dot glow-in-the-dark paint on the outside of your jam jar. Make some dots big and some small – you want it to look like a sky full of stars. You could even look up some constellations to copy if you want it to be really realistic. Let the paint dry, and then when it gets dark eat some yummy snacks by the light of your galaxy and pretend you're in outer space!

Did you know?

Web safe

You can actually buy astronaut food online! Why not visit **www.spacekids.co.uk** and see if there's anything you'd like to try for yourself?

Puzzle and quiz answers

Pages 20–21
London to Rio

1. a 2. b 3. b 4. c 5. c 6. c

Pages 8–11
Detective Brownie:
An ex-CAT science

Puzzle 1: A cat
Puzzle 2: C
Puzzle 3: 364228
Puzzle 4: C
Puzzle 5: BRAIN POWER CAT FOOD
Puzzle 6: B

Pages 12–13
Join the super crew

Aeronautical Engineer – designs and builds rockets and space stations
Astronaut – travels into space to conduct important research
Astrophysicist – studies stars, planets, black holes and all the other mysteries of space
Chemist – investigates the materials that make up our world and their properties
Doctor – specialises in any aspect of the human body to keep people well
Ecologist – studies the relationship between living things and their environment
Forensic Scientist – uses scientific skills to help the police solve crimes
Gemologist – knows all about diamonds, rubies, sapphires and other gems
Geophysicist – studies the Earth using knowledge of gravity, magnetic fields and electricity
Marine Biologist – dives into the oceans to observe sea life
Mechanical Engineer – designs and builds new mechanical systems
Microbiologist – finds out about tiny organisms that cause infections
Nutritionist – knows the right thing to eat for a long and healthy life

Pages 28–29
Words beneath the waves

Something fishy going on...

R	A	E	B	R	E	T	A	W	H
E	H	D	J	U	N	E	M	S	P
W	S	E	A	C	O	W	I	E	R
A	E	S	P	L	O	F	M	A	I
P	A	R	R	O	T	F	I	S	H
E	S	O	S	A	P	P	R	N	E
T	L	H	C	S	E	A	B	A	T
R	U	A	P	E	V	A	W	K	S
C	G	E	N	O	I	L	A	E	S
T	H	S	I	F	G	O	D	N	G

The water bee isn't a real sea animal!

Let's go Began Mob Chic (anagrams)

CUTTLEFISH, BOTTLES, SEAWEED, SANDCASTLE, BUCKET AND SPADE, DRIFTWOOD, FOSSIL AMBERGRIS (whale vomit – eww!)

Say what you sea

1. Seven seas 2. Under the sea
3. Big fish in a small pond 4. Calm before the storm
5. Something fishy about this 6. A drop in the ocean

Palaeontologist – digs for fossils and studies them to learn about evolution
Particle Physicist – researches the basic elements of matter and the forces of nature
Psychologist – studies and treats human behaviour and mental processes
Toxicologist – looks at the impact of poisons and radiation on humans and animals
Volcanologist – specialises in volcanoes and why and when they explode

Pages 42–43
Crime scene investigator

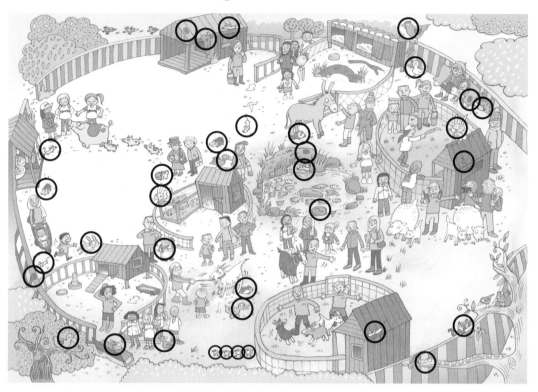

Pages 62–63 Dinosums

Secret sequence

START →	1	1	4	23	34	76	93
12	4	2	6	17	46	80	108
8	5	3	9	21	67	121	163
13	7	10	25	24	35	76	224
21	34	55	89	72	175	49	325
43	76	110	144	100	230	152	647
56	64	134	233	377	610	735	326
80	120	237	476	501	987	863	632

If you arrived at Finish B, relax – you're safe!

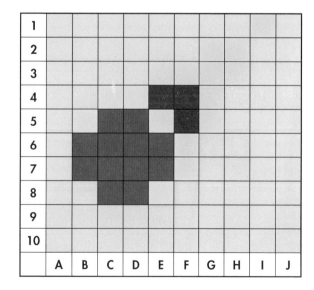

Bones and bits

1. 9 **2.** BONE **3.** CLAW **4.** 3 **5.** BONE

Hid in the grid

It's a meteor – oh no!

Expert escape

Cave 42

Name Colby

Job Operations Manager

'I didn't realise that there are loads of opportunities to work alongside scientists. It is exciting to have a big impact on scientific research without being in a laboratory!'

Fave fact:

'A wound that is bleeding will form a mesh of proteins over the cut. This mesh catches blood cells and hardens. Your body literally makes its own plaster!'

Name Hannah

Job Graduate Engineer

'Get hands on, Brownies! Seeing science at work really helps you understand and also inspires your imagination. Getting on an aeroplane still blows my mind...'

Fave fact:

'The majority of stars you see at night are in fact already dead, because it's taken years and years for that light to reach us.'